THIRD BASE MASTERY

Hot Corner Handbook

Excelling at Third Base

Skills, Strategies, and Secrets

SKY BENSON

TABLE OF CONTENTS

CHAPTER 1

MASTERING THE FUNDAMENTALS

Proper fielding techniques

"And footwork"

The sound of the bat hitting the ball. The noise of the crowd. A fiery line drive sends the ball hurtling toward third base. A skilled third baseman goes from being a blur of motion to a symphony of footwork and technique that ends in a stunning play in that split second. But you don't become a master overnight. Building on good fielding skills and footwork, which are the building blocks of any great defense.

Your ready position is called the "fielding stance.

Think of a spring that is wound up and ready to release its energy. That's what a good fielding position is all about. With your feet shoulder-width apart, your knees slightly bent, and your weight spread out evenly, you can move quickly in any direction. While your back should be straight, it shouldn't be stiff. A slight bend in your back will help you stay balanced and flexible. You hold your hands easily in front of you, palms facing inwards. Your fingers are loose but ready to catch a ball. This balanced, athletic position is where you can start becoming a great fielder.

The Dance of the Diamond is a footwork piece.

Your footwork tells the ball what you want to say. When you get good at it, you can predict, respond to, and block hits that come at you from sharp angles. This is the dance you always do with someone. You stay alert by moving slightly from side to side. This lets you respond to small changes in the batter's swing or the pitcher's delivery. You have to commit when the ball is hit to a particular spot. During the crossover step, you put your other foot across your body, which moves you towards the ball. For ground balls, this is your best move. This is "The Retreat." For fly balls, you need a different pace. It would help if you smoothly stepped back while keeping your balance and your eyes on the ball. Don't forget that small, quick steps work better than long, slow ones.

How to Scoop Ground Balls in the Field

The main thing that a third baseman eats are ground balls. The best part of your footwork and skill is now. Once the ball gets close, take the crossover step to avoid getting hit. Your glove hand should be just below your knee, with your thumb pointing down and the palm of your hand making a pocket. Let the ball fall into the pocket, and then use a smooth, controlled move to pick it up. You don't have to use physical force to catch a ground ball. It's about using your body and glove to form a tube that safely guides the ball into your hands. Head-on, backhand, and forehand are some of the different fielding angles you should work on so you're ready for any case.

Catching fly balls is called "taking flight."

To hit a fly ball, you need to use different skills. Communication is very important here. Make sure you call for the ball clearly so that your teammates don't get confused. As the ball flies, you need to figure out its path and angle. Remember that ignoring a fly ball can cause embarrassing situations and could cost you runs. Keep your place under the ball by taking smooth backpedaling steps. Once you're in place, lift your glove with a strong but loose grip. Let the ball land in your hand without trying to catch it. For better control and smoother movement, try to catch the ball at its highest point instead of a ground ball.

Throwing Techniques

A great field play isn't the whole story. Your throws must hit the runner and be strong to get them out. This is how it breaks down:

The Crow Hop: This is your secret tool for making throws across the diamond. As you grab the ball, move your weight to your back leg with a slight hop forward. This builds up speed for a better throw.

The Motion of Throwing: The important thing is to move smoothly and in sync. Cross your arm over your body so that the elbow is at a right angle to the body. Use your whole body to follow through and turn your energy into the throw.

Building Blocks for Power: Turn your hips and turn your front foot towards the goal as you throw. This makes a strong base for hitting the ball straight.

Practice Makes Perfect: Drills to Improve Your Fielding Skills

It takes hard work and regular practice to become proficient in these methods. Put up cones in different shapes and sizes, and practice shuffling, crossovers, and backpedaling while staying in a catching stance. Have a partner hit ground balls at various speeds and angles while you work on your fielding stance and scooping skills. Toss fly balls at multiple heights and lengths with a partner or use a fly ball machine. Get better at reading the path and making smooth catches. Work on correct mechanics, accuracy, and follow-through by throwing against a wall or with a partner.

Figuring Out What the Hitter Is Thinking

The best third basemen don't just respond; they plan. To guess where the ball might go, learn to read the batter's stance, swing technique, and the situation. Pay attention to how the pitcher throws the ball. A fastball might scream at you, while a breaking ball might tail off. Check the hitter's count. A player who is down in the count might be more likely to go for it, while a player who is up in the count might be trying to get out. As you play more, this feeling of anticipation turns into a sixth sense that helps you get in the right place before the ball is hit.

Getting better at positioning by "Playing the Angles."

Points are everything in third base. You need to be able to change where you are standing depending on the hitter, the situation, and how the pitcher usually throws. When facing right-handed batters, you might move a little closer to the foul line to wait for ground balls to first base. But make changes based on the hitter's power. For example, a pull hitter might need to be positioned lower to stop line drives. If you hit with your left hand, you might want to move a little closer to the line because lefties tend to pull the ball more often. But watch out for hits from the other side, especially from a slap hitter. If there are runners on base, you may need to play less deep to stop them from stealing bases. On the other hand, if there are two outs, you might play lower in hopes of getting a fly ball out.

The Cutoff Man: Putting Together the Outfield Defense

Third basemen are very important because they are the "cutoff man." When a ball is hit into the outfield, you act as a go-between and tell the outfielder which base to throw the ball to for an out. Talking is very important. Make it clear when you want the ball and let the other player know if you'll be making the play or stopping it to throw to another base. Try to guess where the throw will go and get in a position to catch it properly and quickly. This will make sure that the relay goes smoothly and gets the runner out.

Double Play Artistry: How to Turn Two Like a Master

The double play is a beautiful thing, and third basemen are often the ones who lead this symphony of defense. When a runner is thrown out at second base, how you step is very important. As you catch the ball, quickly turn around and throw a laser beam to second to get them out. Do footwork drills to make sure your changes are quick and smooth. Now things get interesting. When the shortstop throws the ball to you for the second out, turn on your back foot and hit a bullet to first base to finish the double play. Speed and precision are very important.

"Mental Toughness: Keeping Your Cool Under Pressure"

It's getting tough. With two outs and the bases full, a hard-hit ball is hit to third base. This is where mental toughness makes the difference between good and great. Picture yourself making tough plays before the game. Imagine being able to handle the ball perfectly, throw strikes, and make crucial double plays. Don't think about the things you did wrong or let the crowd distract you. Keep your mind focused on the next play or ball. Every play gives you a chance to shine. Self-confidence is very important. Believe in your skills, your training, and your gut. No matter how hard it seems, have faith that you can make the play.

It takes time, hard work, and a constant desire to get better to master these advanced methods. But if you practice hard, keep a good mood, and always strive for perfection, you can go from being a good third baseman to a defensive force to be reckoned with. It takes a lot of work to become a great defender, but the rewards are worth it: the thrill of making a play that wins the game and the respect of your friends and opponents.

Developing a strong

"And accurate arm."

A third baseman's best weapon is a strong, accurate arm. It lets you fire rockets across the field, shoot down runners at the plate, and scare the other team's base runners. But getting better at throwing doesn't mean doing mindless exercise or throwing the ball as far as you can. Strength training, proper mechanics, and focused drills are all part of this plan.

Making your throwing strength stronger: "The Powerhouse."

For an arm to be strong, the body must first be strong. This is where lifting weights comes in handy, but don't let the name fool you—it's not just for your arms. Working out different muscle groups to make a strong and balanced throwing motion is like putting together a well-oiled machine. This is what you're built on. When you throw something, a strong core keeps you stable and lets you move power from your legs to your arms. Your core will thank you for doing planks, side planks, and Russian twists. Don't forget about your upper body but work out the right muscles. The muscles that make throwing power stronger can be worked out with dumbbell rows, overhead presses, and external shoulder twists. Your legs power you. When you do squats, lunges, and calf raises, your lower body gets stronger, which makes your throwing move better.

It's important to throw accurately because mechanics matter.

Even though strength is great, it's like having a strong car but a broken gearbox. You can handle things better if you have a comfortable, secure grip. When you play third base, most people use a four-seam grip, which means that the edges of the ball rest across two fingers. Try different things until you find what feels natural and gives you the most power. This is the part where you get ready. Set your feet shoulder-width apart and your weight in the middle of your body. As you wind up, your back leg should straighten out, and your throwing arm should return in a smooth, steady action. Your arm should be across your body, and your elbow should be straight out to the side. Move your energy from your legs to your arm and into the throw as you follow through with your whole body. Pay attention to moving in a coordinated, smooth way and stay away from jerky actions. This is where being exact comes in. When you let go, snap your wrist to give the ball one last burst of speed and spin. For better control, try to let go of the ball at the same point every time.

Working on Your Skills: Arm Drills That Will Shine

It takes work to make your arm strong and effective. Regular practice and targeted drills are needed. This old-school exercise makes your arms stronger and lasts longer. Over time, slowly increase the distance you throw while focusing on smooth movements and accuracy. Start with a partner and a soft throw.

Gradually get farther away and throw harder. Medicine balls add extra resistance to the moving action of throwing. To work out different muscle groups, throw other things, like high throws, chest passes, and rotational throws. This drill helps you work on your throwing skills without a ball. Focus on a smooth windup, follow-through, and release point as you try to throw. Place targets at various distances and work on throwing correctly. Goals can be made with cones, buckets, or even on the wall. This helps you get better at throwing accurately and learn how to throw at different distances.

It's the unsung hero of rest and recovery.

It's hard work to build a strong arm. It takes time for your body to heal and build strength again. Do not work out too hard. When your muscles hurt, you should take a break and let them heal. If you train too much, you could get injured and have to stop. Regular stretching increases your range of motion and flexibility, which can help you throw better and lower your risk of injury. Make sure you give your body the right food. To help your muscles grow and heal, eat a healthy diet that is high in protein. Remember to drink plenty of water—it's essential for good performance.

Getting a strong and effective arm is a process, not a goal. It takes hard work, patience, and a promise to do smart exercise. If you keep working hard, you'll become a formidable defense force. Soon, your throws will be so fast that base runners on the other team will be left shaking their heads, and batters will think twice before going after your arm.

Handling bunts

"And making quick decisions."

There's no doubt that the crack of the bat is the most exciting sound in baseball, but a well-done bunt is also very pretty. It changes the attacking plan and forces the defense to act quickly and decide what to do in a split second. Third basemen need to learn how to handle bunts. You have to show off your speed, fielding skills, and, most importantly, your ability to make quick choices when you're under a lot of stress.

The Bunt Dance: What to Expect from the Play

There are different kinds of bunts. There's the sacrifice bunt, in which the hitter tries to get runners ahead. The hitter hits a slow roller down the line to beat the throw in the drag bunt. There's also the surprise bunt, in which the hitter tries something different that the defense doesn't expect. It's important to be ready. Please pay attention to the score, the number of outs, and the men on base. When there are men on base and less than two outs, a sacrifice bunt is more likely to happen. Look at how the hitter stands and moves. Does a little of their weight move forward? Do they have the bat a little closer to their body? These small clues could mean that someone is trying to bunt. Pay attention to how the pitcher is working the batter. Are they throwing fastballs that move around a lot? Someone at-bat might try to lay down a bunt instead of hitting at a tough pitch.

What to Do About the Bunt: Making the Right Choice

A slow roller comes out when the bat cracks. It looks like time is warping. You need to move quickly and make the right choice at that point. What should you do? Field or Throw? It depends on the case. Fielding the bunt and throwing to the plate might be the best thing to do if there are men on base and no outs at first. With one out at first, though, it might be smarter to throw to get the runner out at second. If you're going to field the bunt, make sure you call it out loud so the pitcher and other infielders don't get confused. That way, no one will throw in a hurry, and the game will go smoothly.

Fielding the Bunt: Speed and Skill

It's all about speed and skill once you decide to field the bunt. Take a quick first step and cross your feet to get in front of the ball. Remember that speed is important, but stay in control and don't dive unless you have to. As the ball gets closer, get down on your knees and scoop the ball up with your glove. Focus on making a pocket with your body and hand to get a good catch. You may need to throw to first or to the plate, depending on the case. It would be best if you practiced throwing from different directions while fielding bunts so that you're ready for anything.

The Force Play: Letting the Runner Go

It's called a force play if you throw to get the runner out at first. When you get close to first base, use a crow hop to pick up speed for a strong throw. Turn around on your back foot and hit first base like a laser. Hold on to your hand and stretch it out towards the base. Put the tag on the base tightly but cleanly as the runner slides or steps on it. Do naming drills to make sure you can do it perfectly.

Practice Makes Perfect: Drills to Master the Bunt

To get good at handling bunts, you have to practice hard. As a "bunt partner," I have a friend who works on laying down bunts in a variety of settings. Pay attention to reading the situation and moving quickly. Hit bunts and throw to first base as practice for force plays. This drill is good for improving your movement, throwing mechanics, and tagging skills. Set up a method where the coach calls for a bunt or a hit. This will force you to act quickly and make the right play. This helps you make better choices when you're under a lot of stress.

Getting into a "Bunt Mentality"

Do more than just drills. Develop a "bunt mentality." Always keep in mind that a bunt could happen and be ready to act right away. Check out professional baseball games and see how different third basemen handle bunts.

Being able to handle bunts well shows how smart you are on defense. It shows how well you can predict what will happen, make quick decisions, and work under pressure. You will go from being a good third baseman to a defensive game-changer if you learn this art.

CHAPTER 2

PLAYING THE HOT CORNER

Strategies for handling

"Hard-hit balls."

The sound of the bat hitting the ball. You are hit by a fiery line drive that looks like a flash of white against the green field. This is what makes the good different from the great: your heart races, and your energy jumps. In that split second, a good third baseman turns into a wall, mastering the art of anticipation and response, ready to calm down a hard-hit ball. Here are some ideas for you to defend yourself against these hot rockets.

Reading the Hitter: A Game of Guessing

Quick reflexes are important not only for dealing with hard-hit balls but also for being ready for them. It would help if you had a good idea of where the ball might be going before you even hit it. Each batter has habits. Watch how they stand, hold the bat, and hit. Does a righty like to pull the ball? Does a lefty really know how to hit line drives? Look at how they did in the past against your team or players like them. Figure out what will happen better if you know more about it. Pay close attention to how the player throws. If the pitch is fast, it might scream at you, but if it breaks, it might go away. A high pitch could lead to a fly ball, while a low pitch could be a laser beam going straight for your zone. A batter who is behind in the count might be going for it, which could lead to a hard-hit ball. On the other hand, a player who has a full count might want to walk, which makes it less likely that the ball will be hit hard.

"Playing the Angles" to Set Yourself Up for Success

Once you know where you think the ball will go, you can set yourself up to win. More and more defensive shifts are being used. As you wait for a ground ball, you might move a little towards first or second base, depending on the hitter, the pitcher, and the situation. But don't get too far out; a well-placed line drive can make things hard for you. You might need to play a little lower to account for possible line drives if the pitcher is known for throwing hard fastballs.

On the other hand, a pitcher who throws a lot of breaking balls might need to be a little deeper to stop ground balls. You might play a little lower with two outs to get under any fly balls, which could be the last out. But if there are men on base, you might need to play deeper to stop possible steals, even if it makes it more likely that the ball will be hit hard.

Footwork Basics: Lightning-Fast Reactions

The ball is hit, and it sounds great. This is where your reflexes and skills will be put to the test. "The First Step" Your first move is significant. Your step should be quick and powerful, ideally a crossing step that sends you in the direction of the ball. Don't be taken off guard; expect to be hit and be ready to act right away. You can shuffle and slide. As the ball gets closer, move your place with a shuffle or a slide. To stay balanced and cover more area, keep your center of gravity low. Don't be afraid to get dirty. A diving stop on a hard-hit ball can make all the difference. If it's a line drive going to the outfield, backpedal slowly and keep your eye on the ball. Remember that controlled, small steps work better than big, lunging ones.

Magic Gloves: Catching the Sizzler

You're in the right place; your footwork is excellent, and you can reach the ball. It's now time for some glove magic. To keep a solid but flexible grip on your glove, make sure you don't squeeze it too hard. You need to be able to bend to follow the ball's path. As the ball gets closer, use your glove to make a pocket. This keeps the ball in your hand and reduces the chance of a pop-out. Do not be afraid to use two hands for hard-hit balls. This makes it more stable and gives you more space to catch the ball.

Better with practice: drills for dealing with heat

It takes consistent practice to become proficient in these methods. Hit fungus with a teacher or use a fungo machine to make it feel like you're being hit hard balls at different speeds and angles. Work on your first step, your footwork, and where you put your hand. Have a partner hit line drives and grounders from different distances and speeds. This lets you work on catching hard-hit balls while your partner acts out a throw or tag. Work on different defensive shifts for different batters and conditions. This enables you to change your position quickly and easily. To make it feel like hard-hit balls that bounce in strange ways, use a spinning machine. This makes it easier to move your hands and eyes together and respond quickly.

Mental toughness

It takes a lot of mental strength as well as physical skill to handle a hard-hit ball. Before the game, picture yourself making plays on balls that are hit hard. Picture yourself responding quickly, getting in the right place, and confidently grabbing the ball. Think back to all the time you spent practicing your footwork and reactions. Believe that you can make the play and trust that you have prepared well. Do not think about the mistakes you made in the past or let the crowd confuse you. Keep your mind focused on the next play or ball. With each ball comes a new chance to shine.

By learning these techniques and building a strong mental game, you'll become a fearless defender who loves being in the heat. Hit hard balls will no longer be a threat but a chance to show how good you are at defense. The crowd's roar as you hit a hot line drive is a sound that you'll never forget. It shows how dedicated, skilled, and brave you are.

Positioning

"And range development."

The third base spot is hard. You connect the infield to the outfield and play a key role in making double plays. You are also the first line of defense against hard line drives. To do well in this job, you need to be very good at positioning and range development. It's important to know where you need to be and when you need to be there, and you need to be able to run a lot.

Understanding Your Zone: Making a Map of the Hot Corner's Area

There is a "zone" for each position, and that is where plays are most likely to happen. As a third baseman, your zone covers a large area. "The Infielder's Depth" means that you'll play closer to the infield than an outfielder would. When there are two outs, you might play deeper to stop fly balls, but when there are runners on base, you might play shorter to prevent bases from being stolen. Your zone is on the right side of the field, just behind first base, and goes to the foul line. But don't be an island; talk to your first baseman and shortstop to make sure there are no gaps in covering. The short outfield on your side is also part of your zone. Get ready to deal with line shots that might go just past the shortstop or first baseman. Remember that talking to the outfielders is very important to avoid confusion and make sure that the cuts are made correctly.

Mastering the Art of Positioning Before the Pitch

It's half the battle to know your zone. Next, you need to get good at pre-pitch positioning, which means putting yourself in the best spot for the case. Does the batter tend to hit the ball to the other side or pull the ball? Look at how they've done in the past and change your stance to match. When facing a pull hitter, you might want to play closer to the line. When facing a slap hitter, you might want to move a little farther out to the outfield. Hitters who have a full count are more likely to walk, which makes it less likely that they will hit a hard ball.

On the other hand, batters who are behind in the count might swing for the fences, which means you need to play a little deeper to account for possible line drives. If there are two outs, catch fly balls first to get the last out. For this, you might need to play a little deeper.

Building your range: making your defensive area bigger

It's important to know where you want to go, but it's also important to have the range to get there. Do drills that make you more agile and help you move laterally. Do drills like shuffles, crosses, and backpedaling to get ready for balls that come at you from different directions. Do plyometric exercises to build rapid power in your legs. This will help you run farther. Box jumps, jump squats, and other plyometric exercises can help you change directions fast and get those balls that are just out of reach. To play defense well throughout the game, you need to have strong legs and a lot of energy. In your workout routine, do running drills and exercises that strengthen your core. Learn to guess where the ball will go after you hit it. This lets you take the best first step and position yourself so you have the best chance of making a play.

Keeping Your Skills Sharp with Situational Drills

Getting better at shooting requires more than just basic drills. Work on different defensive shifts for different batters and situations. This lets you change your position quickly and easily. Have a person hit ground balls at various angles and speeds. You can practice catching the ball and throwing it from different spots in your zone this way. Hit line drives at different heights and angles with a hitting machine, or have a partner do it for you. You can practice backpedaling, following the ball, and diving saves this way.

Communication is Key: Putting the Defense Together

You're not by yourself. To increase your range, you need to be able to communicate clearly. It's essential to be clear with the outfielders when you're calling for fly balls if the ball is clearly in your area. This lets them change where they are standing in case of a cutoff. Talk to the shortstop and first baseman about who will make the tag when you turn a double play. So, there is a smooth shift, and the chance of dropping the ball is low. When the ball is hit to the outfield, you play the role of the "cutoff man" and direct the outfielder's throws to the right base to get out. Make it clear when you want the ball and let the other player know if you'll be making the play or stopping it to throw to another base.

Making things better over and over again

Improving your stance and range is something you do all the time. Every game is different, with new players, events, and odds. Look at game films to find places where you can improve. Look at where you are on various plays and decide if you need to make any changes. Watch skilled third basemen who are known for how well they play defense. Watch how they stand, how they move their feet, and how they deal with different events. Don't avoid hard plays. Think of them as chances to learn and improve your defense skills.

You can go from being a good third baseman to a defensive game-changer by mastering these techniques and staying committed to getting better. Hitters on the other team will have a hard time with your longer range, and your exact positioning will make sure you're always in the right place at the right time to make the play. It's a fantastic feeling when you make a flying stop to prevent a base hit or a perfectly placed backhand throw to catch a runner at first. It shows how dedicated you are to becoming the best third baseman you can be.

Anticipating plays

"And reading hitters."

The sound of the bat hitting the ball is just the start. The real game starts moments before for a good third baseman. Reading the batter, figuring out what the pitcher is trying to do, and guessing where the ball will go before it even leaves the bat is like a mental chess game. Being able to predict and read hitters is what makes a good player great. It turns you from a reactive player into a defense mastermind.

How to Become a Hitter Whisperer

Each hitter has a story to tell, and it's your job to figure it out. A batter's attitude says a lot about them. If you stand wide and put your weight back, you might have a power swing. If you stand narrow and put your weight forward, you might be a contact player who wants to get the ball in play. Watch out for small changes. For example, a batter moving their weight slightly to one side could mean they're going to hit a pull. The way the bat is held gives us important clues. A tight grip could mean that the batter is trying to hit a pull shot to the other field, while an open grip could mean that the batter is attempting to hit a line drive. Watch how they change their grip during the at-bat. For example, a batter who chokes up on the bat might be trying to slide. Look at past results. How has the batter done against pitchers like this one? What are their known tendencies? Do they hit ground balls a lot or fly balls a lot? To get an edge, use scouting reports and research before the game.

Decoding the Pitcher's Story: Figuring Out the Delivery

The thrower is your partner in crime. If you know how they deliver, you can guess how it will affect the batter's approach. Know what the pitcher does well and what they could do better. Is it a fastball that moves quickly or a breaking ball that moves quickly? If the pitcher only throws fastballs, the batter might have to swing early, which makes ground balls more likely.

On the other hand, breaking balls might cause strikes and misses or weak contact. Pay close attention to how the player throws. Are they getting ready to throw a fastball before a curveball? Are they changing speeds to throw off the batter? If you know how the pitcher plans to throw the ball, you can guess how the batter will respond to the next pitch. The hitter's attitude is based on the count. When they are down in the count, they may be bold, swinging for the fences to make it more likely that the ball will be hit hard. If they have a full count, they might want to take a walk, which makes it less likely that they will hit the ball hard.

Putting Expectation into Action: Moving Before the Ball Does

You know what the player is doing, what the pitcher is saying, and what the play will be. Use what you've learned from your analysis to plan where you will be before each throw. This could mean playing farther away for a fly ball or closer to the line for a possible pull hit. Remember that changes are important. Be ready to make small changes based on the batter's body language or the pitcher's windup. Your first move is very important. It should be quick and powerful, and it should ideally be a crossing step that moves you in the direction you think the ball will go. Trust your gut and act right away so you don't get caught off guard. Put your weight low and stay on your toes. This lets you respond quickly to changes in direction and get more done in less time. An even stance also makes you ready for a strong throw or a lunge for a flying catch.

Practice Makes Perfect: Improving Your Ability to Guess

Foresight isn't magic; it's a skill that can be learned. Make drills that look like actual game conditions. As the batter, have a partner take on different stances and swings to show different situations. This helps you get better at reading body language and responding in the right way. Read scouting reports and talk to your coaches about hitter patterns before games. Talk about possible situations and how you might guess how different plays will go based on the information you've gathered. Look at game films and pay attention to plays where preparation made a difference. Look for times when the hitter's body language or the pitcher's delivery could have helped you get in a better position.

The Mental Edge: How to Stay Focused When You're Under Pressure

Don't let other things or the stress of the game make you lose focus. Keep your full attention on the batter, the pitcher, and what's happening in front of you. You've done the work, looked at the data, and have done many tasks. When you're guessing what will happen in a game, trust your gut. The more you do it, the better your skills will get. Everybody messes up sometimes. Look at times when your expectations let you down. Was it the wrong way to read the hitter? A pitch that the pitcher missed? Take what you've learned from these situations and make your next at-bat better.

You can go from being a reactive defender to a creative playmaker by learning how to read hitters and anticipate their moves. You'll be a strong player in the hot corner, stopping the other team's attacks before they even begin. Remember that there is no better feeling than being in the right place at the right time for a play you had been looking forward to. It shows how hard you work, how much you know about the game, and how far ahead of the competition you can think.

CHAPTER 3

OFFENSIVE

CONTRIBUTIONS

Hitting for power

"And average."

When you hit for strength, you can hear the crack of the bat and the cheers of the crowd as the ball soars over the outfield wall. There is, however, another side to the coin: the hitter who hits line shots all over the field and has a high batting average. The best golfer tries to find a balance between these two forces: they want to be able to hit moonshots and keep their contact rate high. Here are some ways to improve your average and power at the plate.

Building a Strong Base: Strength and Technique

To hit hard, you need to start with a strong base. Don't forget how important it is to do strength training. Work on making your legs, core, and upper body more powerful. Do squats, deadlifts, and core routines that move your body in all directions. This strength turns into bat speed, which is the most important thing for making power. Think about how your swing works like a chain. Your legs and core give you control, which moves through your hips and chest to make a strong rotational swing. Pay attention to drills that help your hips rotate properly and move energy around efficiently. Power is exciting, but regular touch is much more critical. Drills like tee work and soft-toss hitting practice can help you get better at controlling your bat. No matter how hard you swing, you should focus on making steady contact with the bat's sweet spot.

How to Find the Sweet Spot in Swing Mechanics

Your swing technique shows you how to do well. A good swing starts with a balanced stance. Keep your feet spaced out so that they feel good. Keep your knees slightly bent and your weight spread out evenly. This balance makes it possible to turn quickly and create power. Try to keep the swing plane level. Do not dip your back shoulder or swing your arms up. A level swing plane makes it easier to make a consistent impact and speeds up the bat as it moves through the hitting zone. Strong follow-through is very important. Do not stop your swing when you hit the ball. Your weight should be on your front leg as you finish your swing. Your front foot should be facing the pitcher. This makes sure that all of your strength goes into the move.

Making smart choices is the hitting approach.

Power and normal don't just have to do with how things work. If the pitch is outside the strike zone, don't chase it. Take your time and wait for a pitch that you can easily handle and hit hard. This makes it more likely that you will make good contact and maybe even hit a home run. Don't just do one thing. Change how you do things depending on what's going on. A well-placed line drive might be more beneficial than a risky swing for a home run when there are men on base. When you get two strikes, you need to protect the plate. Cut down on your swing and concentrate on hitting the ball. This keeps the chance of a blooper or a base hit alive while stopping strikes.

Practice Makes Perfect: Drills for Strength and Speed

Practice every day is the best way to become a well-rounded player. Tee work is one of the most basic drills you can use to improve your bat control and swing techniques. Hit different parts of the tee to make it feel like you're hitting the ball in other places. These drills help you improve your timing and bat speed. During batting practice, the coach throws the ball from a short distance so that you can focus on hitting the ball hard and consistently. Over time, using a weighted bat during batting practice can help you get stronger and faster with the bat. Don't push yourself too hard. Use a weight that lets you use the proper techniques, and then switch to a lighter bat for regular practice. Practice by putting yourself in-game settings. Have your teachers pitch to certain spots or situations to make you make choices at the plate and change how you're hitting the ball.

The Mental Game: How to Stay Focused and Sure of Yourself

Building up your mind is just as important as building up your body. As you think about hitting the ball hard and repeatedly, picture yourself doing it. Picture yourself hitting home runs and line drives all over the field. Visualization boosts confidence and reminds you of the right way to do things. Don't give up when you strike out or get out. Be positive at the plate, pay attention to the next pitch, and believe in how well you've prepared. After the game, look at you're at-bats. Did you hit bad pitches? Were you slow with the bat when the pitch was good? Find ways you can improve and change how you hit in future at-bats.

The Balance Between Power and Average

Any bat will always try to get more power and be more average. Sometimes, it's easy to hit a home run, and other times, a well-placed line drive could win the game. The key is to accept this duality and try to take a well-rounded view of things. Have fun as you learn and improve your hitting skills. Enjoy both the big home runs and the critical hits that win games. Not every player is the same. Some hitters naturally hit for power, while others are great at making steady contact. Find out what your skills and weaknesses are and come up with a plan that makes the most of them. The relievers are throwing harder and with more movement, which means the game is constantly changing. Keep learning the game, get used to different ways of throwing, and change how you hit the ball to match.

Building power and technique, improving your swing mechanics, making intelligent choices at the plate, and training your mind to stay focused will make you a well-rounded hitter who can hit both amazing home runs and game-winning line drives. The crowd's cheers aren't just for the big hits; they're also for the steady, dependable hitters who bring a balanced approach to the plate and help their team win games.

Base running

"And situational awareness."

The sound of the bat hitting the ball. Being on first makes your heart race and your mind blur with excitement. It's time to go. Not only is speed important when running the bases, but you also need to be able to read the situation, guess what will happen, and make quick, smart choices on the bases. When you learn how to run the bases while being aware of your surroundings, you go from being a passive watcher to a powerful force that can steal bases, score runs, and change the outcome of the game.

How to Read the Pitcher: How to Become a Base Running Doctor

It's important to understand the player. Pay attention to how the pitcher winds up. A slow fastball could be indicated by a long, careful windup, which gives you more time to steal. On the other hand, a quick, jerky windup could mean a fastball or breaking pitch, which means you should be more careful. Pay close attention to how the player throws. Does their delivery time change? Does the pitch change where their arm slots? If you know what to expect, these errors can give you chances to steal bases. If the pitcher has a full count, they may be more focused on making a strike than on getting a pickoff. This makes for an excellent chance for a well-timed steal try. On the other hand, if there are no balls in play, the pitcher may be trying to throw over and catch you taking.

The Batter's Box: Figuring Out What They Meant

When it comes to crime, the hitter is your partner in crime. Look at how the batter swings the bat. A big leg kick could mean that the batter will get off to a slow start, giving the runner more time to steal. A quick, tight swing, on the other hand, could mean a faster start, which means you need to be more careful. A batter who is up against a full count is more likely to foul off pitches, which gives the other team a chance to get an extra run or even try to steal. Know what's going on and act in a way that fits the situation. Look at how the batter usually hits. Is it known that they hit ground balls or fly balls? If you know their skills, you can guess where they might hit the ball, which can change your lead and make it easier for them to steal.

The Art of the Lead: Taking Risks (Safely!)

When you have a good idea, you can act right away. Figure out how fast the pitcher throws the ball. If the pitcher throws slower balls, make the lead longer. If they throw fastballs, make the lead shorter. Learn how to do the secondary lead well. At first, take a slight lead, and then, just before the pitcher throws, "rock" back towards the base. This delays the steal attempt, which could catch the defense off guard. Talk to your coach clearly while you're at third base. They see more of the field and can tell you what the best lead size is for your case.

Situational awareness

Base running is like playing chess in your head. These things have a big effect on how active you are. It's a tie game in the bottom of the ninth, and a stolen base could be the game-winner. With two outs in the first inning and a big lead, though, it might be better to be more careful. When there are more than one runner on base, it's important to talk to them. To understand double steals, pickoffs, and possible rundowns, you need to be able to talk to your partners clearly. Look at where the fielders are positioned. Are they going all out? Not deep? Are they ready for someone to try to steal? Based on how the defense is set up, change your plan.

Practice Makes Perfect

Get better at getting leads and figuring out how long the pitcher will throw. Assume that a friend is a pitcher and plays stealing bases with different lead sizes. Learn how to do the head-first slide and the feet-first slide. These tips are very important for safely taking bases and staying healthy. Set up drills that are like the real game. Have a teacher call out situations and have the fielders respond in kind. This will force you to decide whether to steal bases, move forward on ground balls, or tag up on fly balls. Always work hard! On the base tracks, every step you take should have a reason. There's no need to steal a base when you hustle hard. A strong hustle pushes the defense to make perfect throws. Everyone makes mistakes when running bases. Think about times when you were caught stealing or getting thrown out while trying to round a base. Find ways to make things better and learn from your mistakes. On the base tracks, have faith in your skills and follow your gut. You can play with confidence because you know you've worked hard to become a smart and bold base runner.

You'll always be a threat on the base paths if you learn how to run from third base while being aware of your surroundings. You'll get on base, score runs, and make things hard for the other team. The best parts of being a good base runner are the rush of a perfectly timed steal attempt, the thrill of sliding safely into home, and the cheers of the crowd praising your aggression. Your smart and bold base running changed the course of the game, which shows how dedicated you are, how much you know about the game, and how well you can plan.

Bunting

"And other small-ball strategies."

In this day and age of massive home runs and lightning-fast fastballs, it's simple to fall in love with the long ball. Attacking isn't all bad, though. You can also learn how to play small ball. This careful method uses sacrifices, bunts, stolen bases, and smart hitting to make runs one base at a time. To get good at small balls, you need to be precise, disciplined, and know a lot about the game.

A Secret Weapon: The Humble Bunt

The bunt isn't the flashiest move, but it can be used in a lot of different ways. This is the most common type. It moves a runner from first to second by "sacrificing" an out to put another player in score position. When a slow runner is on first and a strong hitter is next, this is very helpful. Hit the ball to first base while running down the line and bunting it. If it's done right, it lets the pitcher get to first base safely and moves any runners up to second. "The Squeeze Play" is a high-stakes play where there is a runner on third base. It's up to the defense to throw home before the runner scores when the batter bunts the ball softly. For this to work, the batter and the runner must communicate and hit at the right time.

Other Small Ball Strategies Besides the Bunt

The bunt is only a part of the small ball puzzle.

Hit and Run: If there is a runner on first, the batter hits at the first pitch, no matter where it is, and the runner tries to steal second base. This can catch the defense off guard and make it easier to score.

The Steal: When you steal bases, the defense has to make perfect throws to keep you out. When done at the right time, a steal can put a runner in a scoring position or even score a run if the throw is dropped.

"Getting Away from the Shift": These days, defenses often use shifts, which put fielders on one side of the infield more than the other, depending on how the batter usually hits. A smart player can take advantage of these changes by hitting the ball to the open side of the field, which makes it hard for the defense to make a play.

The Numbers Game: When the Small Ball Shines

A small ball isn't always a good trick. When facing a strong pitcher, the small ball can help balance out their power. This is especially true when they throw hard and with a lot of movement. You can score runs without relying on power-hitting by getting the ball in play and making the defense make plays. Small-ball plans like the sacrifice bunt or the squeeze play can work very well when there is a runner on base, especially if they are in scoring position. They let you move a runner along and maybe score a run without needing a big hit. It's getting late, and the game is close. Every base and out is very important when the game is close. With steady execution, small ball strategies can help you slow down the game, smartly move runners, and set up scoring chances.

Getting Better at Small Ball: Practice Makes Perfect

To get good at the small balls, you have to work hard and practice. Get better at regularly bunting the ball to different parts of the field. Pay attention to where you put your hands and how you handle the bat for accurate execution. In "Sacrifice Bunt Situations," Set up drills where there is a runner on first and an out, just like in a game. Bunting is a way to move the runner forward while making sure you get out safely. Hit fake shifts to get better at it. This will teach you how to hit the ball to open parts of the field and help you recognize different shift alignments.

The Small Ball Mindset: Discipline and Being Aware of Your Environment

Making smart choices and carrying them out perfectly is what small ball is all about, not flashy plays. Don't hit everything that comes your way. Be calm and wait for the right pitch to hit the ball and move runners forward. Situational awareness means knowing what's going on in the game and what could happen with each play. Pick the small ball strategy that works best for you and gives you the best chance of winning. Teamwork is very important in small balls. Talk to your teammates, know what they need to do to make the play work, and perform with precision to get the most out of it.

You'll be very helpful to your team if you learn how to play small ball. You'll be the player who knows how to read the situation and uses a variety of strategies to get the ball into play, move runners in a way that makes sense, and eventually create chances to score. You'll be the kind of baseball player who knows that hitting home runs isn't enough to win. You'll also see that you need to use every offensive tool you have to beat the other team. The beauty of a small ball is how well it works. It doesn't take brute force; all you need is a well-coordinated team, the ability to plan, and the accuracy to carry out your plans. Only in baseball can you feel the thrill of winning a close game with a perfectly put bunt or a hit-and-run at the right time. It shows how dedicated your team is to the basics, how well you can change, and how well you understand that the best offenses are sometimes the smallest.

CHAPTER 4

THE MENTAL EDGE

Staying focused

"In high-pressure situations."

With two outs in the bottom of the ninth, the bases are full. As you walk up to bat, the loud noise of the crowd hits you like a wave. It feels like the weight of the game is on your shoulders, and you can feel every move the pitcher makes and every call the judge makes. This is where the mind game makes the difference between good and great. Here's how to get the laser focus you need to do well on the baseball pitch when things get tough.

Taming the Inner Beast: How to Deal with Anxiety

Getting anxious is a normal reaction to stress. Take slow, deep breaths when you feel the tension rising. Pay attention to your breathing to calm your body and mind and keep stress from getting in the way of your decisions. Get rid of the lousy self-doubt. Say something positive instead, like "I've trained for this" or "I trust my abilities." Talking positively to yourself boosts your confidence and gives you the tools you need to win. Picture yourself winning. Picture yourself hitting the ball hard, making a play in the field, or throwing a perfect strike. Visualization trains your brain to do well and lowers your stress by getting your mind ready for stress.

Keeping Your Focus: Tuning Out the Noise

When things are tough, the world can seem to get smaller. Don't think about how the game turned out or the noise from the crowd. Instead, concentrate on the job at hand. For a batter, it could mean paying attention to how the bowler throws the ball. In the case of a fielder, it could be reading the batter's move. Do something before you pitch or play that helps you focus. To do this, you could take a few deep breaths, change your position, or picture yourself succeeding. A routine gives you a sense of control and clears your thoughts of things that aren't important. There are a lot of hours of practice that have helped you get better at the game. When things are stressful, trust your gut. Do not overthink; instead, act naturally and depend on what you have learned.

Take on the Challenge: Turning Pressure into Opportunity

It would help if you did not fear pressure; instead, see it as a chance to do your best. Stress shouldn't be seen as a burden but as a task. Take advantage of the chance to show off your skills and show how tough you are. This change in how you think about things can turn your worry into a force that helps you do better. Don't focus too much on how the game turns out. You should pay attention to the process, like the physics of your swing, the basics of fielding, and how you throw the ball. Focusing on the here and now keeps you from getting too stressed out about the bigger picture. Have faith in yourself. Believe in how well you've prepared, your skills, and your ability to do well under stress. Being able to stay focused and do your best when it means most depends on how much you believe in yourself.

"Building Mental Toughness

It takes time to become mentally tough. Practice being under pressure like you are in a game. Set up challenging situations with men on base and two outs with the coaches' help. Reliving these events helps you learn how to handle your feelings and concentrate when things get tough. Picture yourself doing well in stressful situations on a regular basis. If you picture success very clearly, you'll be better ready to handle it when it comes true. Think about times when you were under a lot of stress in the past. What did well? How could you have done it better? Learning from both wins and losses makes you mentally stronger and helps you improve how you play in future games.

Focusing when you're under a lot of stress is a skill that you need to keep working on and dedicate yourself to. If you learn these methods and work on your mental toughness, you'll go from being a player who gives up when things get tough to one who is unstoppable when the game is close. In baseball, the most memorable times often happen when there is a lot of pressure. You can seize those chances and write your part in baseball history if you stay focused and believe in your skills.

Building confidence

"And resilience."

There are highs and lows in baseball. One day, you'll hit massive home runs, and the next, you'll strike out looking. It's not just physical skill that makes you successful; it's also your mental toughness, like how confident and strong you are. These traits give you the strength to get back on your feet after a loss and perform at your best, even when it seems like the odds are against you. Here's how to get more confident and tough on the baseball pitch:

Having confidence is the key to success.

Having confidence means you believe you can do well. Don't play down what you've done well. Enjoy your wins, no matter how big or small they are. A game-winning hit, a perfect inning of pitching, or an amazing diving catch are all things that should be praised. Enjoy the thrill of winning, and let it give you courage for future games. Everybody has good and bad points. Figure out what your strengths are as a player and use them to your benefit. Do you have a strong swing? A quick runner on base? Someone with a sharp mind? Work on these skills and believe in your ability to use your unique strengths to help the team. Stop being so hard on yourself. Instead, to improve your mood, use positive mantras. Say to yourself, "I am ready" or "I trust my skills" before a game. Positive self-talk helps you feel good about yourself and fights self-doubt.

Resilience: Getting Back on Your Feet After a Setback

Everybody messes up sometimes. Being resilient means being able to learn from mistakes and get back up stronger. Don't think about mistakes all the time. Look at what went wrong. Did the pitch you hit not work? Do you miss a catching play? You should find the mistake, learn what caused it, and then let it go. Focus on what you're learning and how you can use it in your next at-bat or receiving chance. Don't see loss as a dead end; see it as a way to get to the next step. You can learn and get better from every mistake. Setbacks can help you figure out how to get better, so commit to becoming a better player. Spend time with people who are good for you. You can watch videos of great baseball players getting through tough times or talk to teachers and mentors who can give you advice and support.

Developing a Growth Mindset: Taking on Challenges

A growth mindset is the idea that you can get better at things by working at them and practicing them. Not being afraid of difficulties is good. Try new things and get out of your comfort zone. You could work on hitting with a heavier bat, handling drills that require you to be more agile, or trying out different ways to throw the ball. Taking on tasks helps you learn new skills and improve the ones you already have, which also boosts your confidence. Focusing too much on the end result can make you angry. Pay attention to the process: your commitment, hard work, and constant progress. Celebrate small wins, like getting better at a new skill or raising your hitting average. Enjoy the process of getting better as a player, and the confidence will come on its own. You can always learn something new when you play baseball with other people. Watch how your coworkers deal with stress and how they learn from their mistakes. Share your stories with them and learn from each other.

Building Strong Support Systems: A Group Task

It takes more than one person to build faith and resilience. Look for coaches who have faith in you and will push you to do your best. They'll be happy for your wins, give you helpful feedback, and help you figure out how to deal with problems. When teammates become family, your friends are a big part of what keeps you going. Cheer each other on, enjoy your wins, and help each other get back up after you lose. A strong team bond makes you feel like you are fit and makes you stronger mentally. Keep around you positive people, like family, friends, and teachers, who believe in you and give you support.

Strengths like confidence and toughness need to be worked out all the time. If you focus on the process, enjoy your wins, learn from your losses, take on challenges, and surround yourself with positive people, you'll build the mental strength to do well on the baseball field, even when things get tough. You can take on any task and write your own baseball story if you have a strong mind and a strong spirit.

Leading by example

"And being a team player."

People often romanticize baseball as a sport with lone stars. But the truth is that one-person shows don't usually win titles. Teams that have strong guidance and always work together are the ones that do the best. Find out how to be the player who has both traits and is the heartbeat of your team on and off the pitch.

As an example, show more than just facts.

Being a leader is more than just having a title or a captain's band. It's about showing your friends how to act by the way you act. Show how dedicated you are by getting to practice early and staying late to work on your skills. The way you work sets an example for your teammates and motivates them to do their best. Don't hold back, whether it's a simple grounder or a run for an extra base. Your never-ending drive shows your partners that every play is critical and inspires them to match your intensity. Even when things aren't going your way, keep in a good mood. Keep your team spirit high by cheering them on and forgiving them when they make a mistake. A positive leader makes the workplace a place where everyone feels appreciated and supported.

"We" are more important than "me" when it comes to being a team player.

You must put the needs of the team ahead of your own if you want to be a team player. Everyone on the team has a job to do, from the best hitter to the best defender. Accept your job, get good at what you do, and focus on helping the team succeed, not on your own glory. Talk to your friends, share information with them on the field, and speak up as a leader at bat and in the dugout. Making sure everyone is on the same page through clear conversation cuts down on mistakes. Be truly pleased for your friends' successes. You should be very happy when a partner hits a home run or makes a great defensive play. This builds team spirit and makes the tie between team members stronger.

The Power of Positive Influence: Getting Your Teammates to Do Better

Leadership and working together go beyond what you do on the pitch. Do not only be a good player but also a good teammate. Get to know your teammates' personalities, skills, and weaknesses. This helps people feel like they belong and builds a strong team atmosphere. If you see someone having a hard time in practice or feeling down after a bad game, give them a boost or a hand. Being a helpful partner makes everyone feel better and makes the team work better as a whole. Everybody messes up sometimes. If you mess up, admit it and try to make things right. Taking responsibility builds trust and shows that you want the team to succeed.

It's not about awards when you lead with your heart.

Getting awards and praise isn't really what leading is all about. It means getting your partners to be their best on and off the pitch. A winning culture is made up of people who are dedicated, positive, and helpful. Everyone can grow and reach their full potential in this positive setting. It's more satisfying to win with other people. A deeper and longer-lasting feeling of accomplishment comes from knowing that you helped the team win as a whole. The lessons learned about working together, talking to each other, and being responsible can be used in all parts of life. That's right, you'll become a better boss, teammate, and person all around.

It takes time and work to become a leader and a great team player. If you show these traits, you'll go from being just another player to being the heart and soul of your team. Your friends, coaches and anyone else who sees how dedicated you are to the game and your team will remember you for a long time.

CHAPTER 5

STRENGTH AND CONDITIONING

Tailored workouts

"For third basemen."

Strong upper and lower body muscles are essential for a well-rounded third baseman. For handling plays and throws, the core needs to be stable and able to rotate. Squats are a basic workout that works your core, glutes, and legs. You can squat with barbells, bars, or even your own body weight. You work your hamstrings, hips, and lower back when you deadlift. Start with small weights and add more as you get stronger. Lunges are a great way to work your hips, hamstrings, and quads. You can do side lunges, forward lunges, or backward lunges. Push-ups are a well-known way to work out your chest, shoulders, and arms. Change them up by doing them on your knees if you need to. Pull-ups are a great way to work out your back and arms. Use a machine that helps you do pull-ups if you need to. You can use a barbell or dumbbell for the overhead press, which works your shoulders and arms. Use a barbell, dumbbell, or a rowing machine to work on your back and arms.

Exercises that use plyometrics to build explosive power

For third basemen who need to jump and throw fast, plyometrics are a great way to build explosive power. Box jumps are a great way to make your legs stronger. As you get stronger, slowly raise the height of the box from low to high. To do depth jumps, find a stable platform about knee-high and jump down from it. Then, jump back up quickly. To get faster, jump from side to side as fast as you can.

Heart and Blood Pressure Endurance

All baseball players need to do cardio, but third basemen need it the most because they have to run long distances and recover quickly. You might want to include things like short sprints, long lengths, or interval training to make your heart and lungs stronger. Biking is a good way to get cardio without hurting your joints. Swimming is another great low-impact way to get some exercise.

Drills Just for Baseball

You can do these drills by yourself or with a teacher to improve your footwork, hand-eye coordination, and throwing accuracy. You can do these drills by yourself or with a coach to improve your arm strength and throwing technique. Work on your hitting with a teacher or by yourself.

This is only a hint. Pay attention to your body and rest when you need to. If you train with these things in mind, you'll be well on your way to becoming a solid and skilled third baseman!

Flexibility

"And injury prevention."

At third base, a screaming line drive comes straight at you. You lunge, grab the ball with a glove that's just barely bigger than the fast-moving object, and throw it to first base with all your might, getting the out. A great third baseman makes plays like this that are smooth, strong, and look like they come naturally. But this show of speed hides a secret weapon: the ability to bend and stretch.

The Advantage of Flexibility for Third Basemen

You need to be able to move your hips, knees, legs, and shoulders a lot when you dive, stop, leap, catch, or twist throw. If your body is flexible, you can reach farther, bend deeper, and twist into poses that a stiff player would not be able to do. Every instant counts when a ball is hurtling at you. Tight muscles can make it harder to react because your body has to work harder to move. Being more flexible makes your reflexes and transitions faster and smoother, giving you that important edge in the game. Tears and strains are more likely to happen in muscles that are tight, especially when playing third base and making quick moves. Regular stretching helps keep your muscles loose and flexible, which lowers the chance of getting hurt and ruining your season. Being flexible makes your blood flow better all over your body, which brings essential nutrients to your muscles and joints. This increased blood flow helps you heal faster from games and practices, so you always feel ready to perform.

Putting flexibility first

For these stretches, you move in a way that is similar to what you do on the pitch. Do lunges with arm circles, high knees, and rotating your torso to warm up your muscles and get them ready for exercise. To lengthen and open up specific muscle groups, hold these stretches for a long time (usually 30 seconds). Pay attention to your chest, legs, quads, glutes, hip flexors, and shoulders. These methods use moves and exercises that you can do with your own body to make you more flexible, strengthen your core, and improve your balance. One or two times a week, you might want to do yoga or Pilates.

To make being flexible a habit, you need to be consistent.

Stretch for at least 10 to 15 minutes after every workout, focusing on the main muscle groups you used during practice. Do not work out too hard. It should be nice to stretch, not painful. Don't stretch if it hurts. Instead, talk to a trainer or sports doctor. Make sure you're stretching correctly to keep yourself from getting hurt. Ask a trainer or guide to show you how to do each stretch correctly.

A Whole-Body Approach to Avoiding Injuries

Even though flexibility is very important, it's not the only thing that can help you avoid getting hurt. Stretching and light cardio should always be done before training and games to get your body ready to move. Afterward, cool down with static stretches to help your body heal. Having strong muscles makes your joints more stable, which lowers your risk of getting hurt. To keep your body from getting too stressed, make sure you wear shoes that fit well and use the right gear when you practice. Staying hydrated keeps your muscles working right and lowers the chance that they will hurt. During the day, drink a lot of water. Take care of your pain. Take a break or see a doctor if you're feeling uncomfortable. When you try to push through pain, you can hurt yourself more.

By putting flexibility first and following these tips for avoiding injuries, you'll be well on your way to becoming a third baseman who not only makes fantastic plays look effortless but also stays healthy and plays all season. A flexible body is also strong and durable, which is important for a long and successful baseball career.

Nutrition

"And recovery strategies"

Third basemen are in the middle of all the action in baseball, which is a challenging game. When you dive to catch something or throw something really hard, your body needs the right food to work at its best and recover quickly. Here are some tips on how to improve your diet and recovery to become a stronger and more durable third baseman.

How to Build a Champion's Plate: The Power of Good Nutrition

The food you eat gives your body most of its energy. These provide you with energy that lasts all game. Pick whole grains like quinoa, brown rice, and whole-wheat pasta. Fruits and veggies are also great places to get essential vitamins and complex carbs. Protein is vital for growing muscle and fixing damage to it. Grilled chicken, fish, beans, and lentils are all lean protein sources that you should eat. Do not be afraid of good fats. In addition to helping your body absorb nutrients, they also help make hormones and make you feel fuller for longer. Choose foods like avocado, nuts, seeds, and fatty fish.

Pre-Game Meals: Getting Ready to Perform

A meal before a game sets the tone for how well you do. Eat your meal two to three hours before the game. This gives your body time to break down the food and turn it into energy. Eating a meal with complex carbs like brown rice and veggies and lean protein like grilled chicken will give you energy that lasts all game and keeps you feeling strong. Before the game, make sure you drink a lot of water. Aim for 16 to 20 ounces of water two to three hours before the game, and keep drinking water all day.

Meals after a game: replenishing and rebuilding

The repair work begins as soon as the game is over. Try to eat a meal to help your body heal within 30 to 45 minutes of the game. This is the best time for your body to absorb nutrients. Make sure you get a mix of complicated carbs and lean protein. A great choice is grilled chicken or fish with brown rice or sweet potatoes. Keep drinking water after the game. A sports drink or water with electrolytes can help you get back to normal and replace minerals you've lost.

Beyond Meals: Strategies for Recovering for Peak Performance

What you eat is only one part of getting better. Don't wait until you're thirsty to drink water. Drinking water at regular times throughout the day helps your body work at its best and keeps you refreshed. Aim to get at least 7-8 hours of good sleep every night. Sleep is essential for recovery and efficiency because it lets your body repair and rebuild muscle tissue. As a form of active recovery, doing light activities like yoga or walking on your days off can help your muscles repair and keep you from getting stiff.

It's important to stretch and foam roll. Stretching regularly makes you more flexible and lessens muscle pain. Foam rolling can help you work on specific muscle groups and speed up the healing process of tissues.

Listen to Your Body: Fueling for Your Own Needs

Everybody has a different body. Writing down what you eat in a food book can help you figure out patterns in your eating that affect your energy and performance. A registered dietitian can make a custom nutrition plan for you that takes into account your needs, body type, and level of exercise. You should pay attention to how different things make your body feel. Try different meals before and after the game to see what works best for you.

It will be easy for you to become a powerful force at third base if you give your body the proper nutrients and use good recovery techniques. A body that is well-fed and rested is strong and ready to make the plays that win the game and help your team win.

CHAPTER 6

THE GAME PLAN

Pre-game preparation

"And scouting."

It's game day. There is the crack of the bat and the roar of the crowd. Today is the day for stars to rise. But as a third baseman, you need to do some essential things before you step onto the pitch. Learn how to study and prepare for games before they happen, and you'll go from being a good player to a game-changing force at the hot corner.

Getting Ready for the Game: Sharpening Your Tools

A good game starts a long time before the first pitch. Get to the pitch early to warm up properly. You can get your body ready for the quick moves you'll need on the field by doing light exercises, dynamic stretches, and throwing drills. Close your eyes and picture yourself making plays, like throwing strikes to first and fielding grounders easily. Visualizing something in your mind helps you stay focused and boosts your trust in your skills. Talk to your coaches and players about the hitters on the other team. Talk about how to set up your defense, how to run the bases, and possible problems you might face. Cut down on distractions. Don't think about bad things, put your phone away, and concentrate on the job at hand. With this sharp focus, you'll be able to act naturally on the pitch.

Scouting Reports: Taking the Mystery Out of the Opposition

It's half the fight to know who your opponent is. To understand the batters, read the spy reports on the other team's batters. Look at how they hit the ball when they're at bat. Do they pull hits or throw the ball all over the pitch? Being aware of their skills and weaknesses lets you plan for their swings and place yourself correctly. Put yourself in front of each hitter. Think about how they swing, what they do when the ball is pitched differently, and where they might hit it. This helps you get ready for different situations and respond naturally to the pitcher-hitter battle. Don't just focus on how to swing. Does it happen often that they steal bases? Do people know them for bunting? If you know these habits, you can better guess what they'll do next and make important plays.

Beyond the Basics: More Advanced Scouting Tips

There are more things to scout than just notes. If you can, watch videos of the last few games that the other team played. Watch how the batters approach the ball, how they swing, and how they respond to different pitches. Talk to the players you have. Talk about their game plan for each hitter, including where they like to hit the ball and what pitches they plan to throw. If you know their plan, you can guess where they will hit the ball and set yourself up so you have the best chance of making a play. If you can, watch the other team bat during batting practice. Find patterns and weak spots, and then use what you've learned to improve your defense position.

Putting what you know into practice

Scouting is pointless if you don't use what you learn. Tell your teammates what you've learned from scouting. Talk about how to set up your defense, how to run the bases, and possible problems you might face. This way of working together makes your general defensive strategy stronger. Baseball moves quickly. Watch how the batters respond to pitches as the game goes on and make changes to where you are standing or how you talk to the other fielders based on what you see. Trust your gut after checking out everything and getting ready. You can stop the other team by acting quickly, making smart plays, and relying on your skills and knowledge.

Preparing for games and planning are very important for a third baseman to do well. When you combine a thorough warm-up practice with a thorough knowledge of your opponent, you'll go from being an observer to changing the game. When you put what you know into action, it can change the game and help your team win.

In-game strategies

"And adjustments."

The crowd roars and the bat cracks. The game has begun! As a third baseman, you're right in the middle of everything. But even the best-laid plans made during planning and getting ready for the game can change in an instant. Here's how to change your plans quickly, go with the flow of the game, and become the best at the hot corner.

Reading the Hitter: More Than Just a Scouting Report

You can learn a lot from scouting reports, but they're not perfect. Listen to the batter's position, where they put their weight, and how they hold the bat. They may use subtle cues to show whether they want to hit hard, make contact, or lay down a ball. Is there a specific pitch the hitter wants? Are they more likely to hit a home run or take a walk when the pitch count is high? If you know the pitch count, you can guess when they will come in. Is there a runner on first? Two outs? When you know what's going on, you can change where you are based on what play you might need to make.

Working together to communicate with your team

Connect with your player through silence. You can tell the batter about your favorite positions or defensive shifts without giving them away by making eye contact, nodding your head, or sending pre-programmed signals. After a fly ball, let the outfielders know where the ball might land and how it will likely be caught. This makes sure the change goes smoothly and lowers the chance of mistakes. As the play goes on, make clear calls to help your friends follow along. A "Ball!" signal means a fly ball, and a "Short!" or "Home!" command makes sure that everyone is on the same page.

Getting Used to the Game: Being Flexible

A batter who was going for home runs at first might change their strategy for a late-inning hit. You should be ready to change your position as things change. A strong wind can make a fly ball go out of play or move a grounder farther. Change the depth of your playing based on the direction and strength of the wind. Are you ahead by one run in the late innings of the game? Be safe and move deeper to avoid a double that would tie the game. Down by more than one run? Try a flying catch to get people to cheer.

Mental Toughness

Please "Shake it Off" and don't let mistakes pile up. Take a deep breath, learn from your mistake, and get back to the next play. Not moving on from the past only slows you down. A good mood spreads like wildfire. Keep the energy up, cheer on your friends, and remember that the game isn't over yet. You worked hard at practice. Believe in your gut, depend on your skills, and be sure of yourself before every play.

You'll be a great third baseman who can handle any situation, stop the other team's offense, and help your team win if you learn how to communicate, make changes during the game, and keep your cool. Because the game is like a dance, you need to be able to respond and change to make a difference on the pitch.

Communication

"And working with pitchers."

A third baseman and a pitcher work together like a quiet symphony on the baseball field. If you can't talk to each other clearly, a well-thrown pitch can become an annoying mistake, and a grounder that seems normal can turn into a double that changes the game. Here's why this dynamic pair needs to talk to each other:

Building Trust

The pitcher and third baseman should be able to trust and understand each other. If you know the pitcher's favorite pitch for a particular situation, you can guess how the batter will react and move your body to match. A defensive shift may be used against some batters. Talking about the change ahead of time makes sure that everyone is on the same page, which reduces confusion and increases the chances of a good play. Learn a silent language of head nods, hand gestures, or pre-set signs that you can use to tell the pitcher where to throw the ball or make defensive changes without giving the batter away.

Reading the Game Together

Good conversation is more than just talking before a game. The two players should be aware of how the other person is moving. A quick look from the pitcher can let you know what pitch is coming, and a subtle hand signal from the third baseman could mean that the reference needs to change for the next hitter—talk based on what's going on in the game. In the late stages, you're ahead by one run. To stop a double that would tie the game, you might ask for a deeper spot. Down by more than one run? To start a gathering, a more aggressive stance might be needed. A short chat can be very helpful after a play. Did you expect the game to be somewhere else? Did the ground ball jump out of the blue? Both the pitcher and the third baseman can change how they play for the next batter after sharing these thoughts.

"The Voice on the Field"

When a fly ball is hit, the third baseman tells the outfielders where the ball might land and how far it went. This makes sure the change goes smoothly and cuts down on mistakes. The third baseman leads his friends with clear calls as the game goes on. Everyone is on the same page when you call "Ball!" for fly balls and "Short!" or "Home!" to lead your teammates.

The pitcher and third baseman go from being separate players to working as a team by building a strong communication link. This leads to smooth plays, a disappointed offense, and more wins for your team in the end.

Closing Thoughts

There you have it! This guide has taught you a lot of valuable things that will help you become a great third baseman. This is only the beginning of your baseball journey. You have to keep learning new things, getting better at old ones, and adjusting to new situations. Be a leader, not just a player. Set a good model for your teammates. Set the tone for the team's success by being dedicated, working hard, and having a good mood.

Embrace the hard work. Dedication is very important, both on and off the pitch. Training regularly, eating right, and taking time to rest will help you stay healthy, strong, and ready to do your best. Get good at the basics. A strong throwing arm, good footwork, and smooth fielding movements are what make a great third baseman. Don't stop getting better at these critical skills. The game is a puzzle for your mind. Learn to read the situation, talk to your friends clearly, and change your plans based on the batter, the pitcher, and the game as a whole.

Don't just respond; think too. "Love the game." Passion drives your commitment. Why you started playing: the thrill of the game, the friendship with your teammates, and the pure joy of making a play that changes the outcome of the game. Baseball is a hard sport, but it's also an enjoyable one. You can go from being a good third baseman to a truly dominant force by putting in the work, taking on the task, and developing a love for the game. Every great player had to start somewhere. This is your chance to play, write your own story, and make your mark on the game. We hope everything goes well for you in baseball! As you continue to work on your skills and follow your dreams in the field, we hope this guide is helpful.